I0453297

One-Way Relationships

The Path to Joy, Resilience, and Wholeness

Hope ✒ Grace
P U B L I S H I N G
Alexandria, Virginia, USA

By Hope Grace

Published by Hope Grace Publishing
HopeGracePublishing.com
Alexandria, Virginia, USA

This book is a work of nonfiction. While the author has made every effort to ensure accuracy and clarity, some names, details, and events have been changed to protect the privacy of individuals. Any resemblance to actual persons, living or dead, is purely coincidental.

ISBN: 978-1-966423-14-0 (Paperback)
ISBN: 978-1-966423-15-7 (Hardback)
ISBN: 978-1-966423-16-4 (ebook)
Library of Congress Control Number:
2024926478

First Edition: 2025

Dedication

To everyone searching for joy, resilience, and
wholeness.

May you discover the transformative power of
one-way love.

Contents

Practical Exercises: Ideas for readers to practice one-way relationships in various areas of their lives.

Introduction: The Freedom of Giving Without Expecting

In a world where relationships are often seen as transactions — a constant balancing act of giving and receiving — the idea of a one-way relationship can feel foreign, even radical. A one-way relationship defies the conventional expectation of reciprocity. It is love or kindness extended freely, without strings attached, and without the need for acknowledgment or repayment. Instead of operating on the principle of "I'll do this for you if you do something for me," one-way relationships are built on unconditional giving.

This concept is countercultural in many societies, including my own Chinese heritage, where relationships are often measured by the balance of favors and obligations. In my early years, I understood love and kindness as investments that should yield a return. If my efforts were ignored or unreciprocated, it was easy to feel hurt, slighted, or even resentful. It wasn't until I encountered the teachings of Jesus Christ that my perspective began to shift. I learned that giving doesn't have to depend on the response of the receiver; it can instead flow from the abundance of the giver's heart.

I'll never forget the moment when this truth truly resonated with me. Years ago, when my family and I attended a Bible study in a small home, I saw a glimpse of this radical love in action. The hosts had opened their doors to strangers, offering food, warmth, and wisdom without expecting anything in return. At first, I took their generosity for granted, assuming it was their role to provide. But as I grew in my faith, I began to see the depth of their sacrifice. They gave joyfully, not out of obligation, but because their love was rooted in their faith in Christ. Watching them give so freely and selflessly changed something in me. I realized that their joy didn't come from what they received but from what they gave. This shift in mindset was liberating. It freed me from the heavy burden of unmet expectations and the emotional toll of unreciprocated kindness. I began to see that the act of giving itself can be deeply fulfilling

— an expression of faith, a reflection of God's grace, and an opportunity for personal growth.

In this book, I want to explore what it means to live a life grounded in one-way relationships. From personal stories to biblical insights, I'll share how embracing this mindset has transformed my understanding of love, relationships, and even my own identity. I'll discuss the challenges and rewards of giving unconditionally and offer practical ways to incorporate this philosophy into your everyday life.

At its heart, this book is about freedom — the freedom to love without limits, to give without fear, and to live a life of abundance rooted in grace. By embracing one-way relationships, we are not only following the example of Jesus but also unlocking a profound source of joy and peace.

This journey may challenge your assumptions about relationships, just as it did mine. But I believe that as you read these pages, you'll discover the beauty of loving unconditionally — not because it benefits you, but because it reflects the love you've already received.

Part I: Understanding One-Way Relationships

Chapter 1: Cultural Contexts: Reciprocity vs. Grace

Relationships often reflect the values and traditions of the cultures in which they are formed. In Chinese culture, the foundation of relationships lies in reciprocity — a deeply ingrained expectation that favors, kindness, and gifts must be balanced. This cultural practice, often referred to as *guanxi*, is a network of mutual obligations where the giving and receiving of help or resources are meticulously tracked. It's a system that fosters social harmony and accountability, but it also binds relationships to a ledger of debts and repayments.

Growing up in China, I was taught that every act of kindness carried an implicit expectation of repayment. A neighbor's loan of sugar was not a simple favor; it came with the understanding that you would return the favor at an appropriate time. Even in friendships and family relationships, giving and receiving were rarely unconditional. This mutual exchange, while practical, often blurred the lines between genuine care and transactional obligation. It created a sense of security, but also an undercurrent of pressure. Relationships became a balancing act, and failure to reciprocate could lead to tension, mistrust, or even estrangement.

I saw this dynamic play out countless times. In my early days in America, I introduced Henry, a fellow student from China, to a local church and gave him a bilingual Bible as a gift. His hesitation to accept it revealed this cultural mindset. He asked, "How can I ever repay you?" His question wasn't just a polite expression of gratitude — it was a genuine concern. In his mind, accepting my gift meant incurring a debt he would someday have to repay. This deeply ingrained cultural expectation made the concept of unconditional giving foreign, even unsettling.

It wasn't until I became a Christian that I began to see relationships differently. The idea of grace, central to the Christian faith, stood in stark contrast to the reciprocity I had known all my life. Grace is the unmerited favor of God — a gift freely given, not because we have earned it, but because God's love for us is unconditional. This radical concept flipped my understanding of relationships upside down. Grace taught me that love doesn't have to be earned or repaid; it can simply be given, without expectation.

The principle of grace is woven into the fabric of Christian teachings. The Apostle Paul writes in Ephesians 2:8-9, *"For it is by grace you have been saved, through faith — and this is not from yourselves, it is the gift of God — not by works, so that no one can boast."* Grace is a gift that cannot be earned, and it invites us to extend the same unconditional love to others.

At first, this idea was difficult to reconcile with my upbringing. I wrestled with questions like: "What if my love is taken for granted? What if I get hurt?" These fears are natural, and they reflect the protective instincts ingrained in us by a culture of reciprocity. But as I grew in my faith, I began to see that the freedom of giving without expecting was worth the risk. When love is offered without strings attached, it creates space for relationships to flourish without the weight of obligation or resentment.

This shift in perspective doesn't mean abandoning cultural traditions entirely. Reciprocity can have its place in fostering community and mutual care. However, when it becomes the sole basis for relationships, it limits the capacity for genuine, selfless love. Grace offers a new way — a way that liberates both the giver and the recipient from the burden of expectation.

Reflecting on my journey, I see how grace transformed my understanding of relationships. It taught me that love is most powerful when it is given freely, not as a transaction, but as a reflection of the love God has shown us. As Christians, we are called to be vessels of this grace, extending it to others, even when it defies cultural norms or personal instincts. Through grace, I learned that the value of a relationship isn't measured by what we receive in return, but by the joy of giving itself. This joy is not diminished by a lack of reciprocity; instead, it is deepened by the freedom to give without fear or expectation. Grace replaces the ledger of debts and repayments with an open invitation to love unconditionally, just as we have been loved.

Chapter 2: Biblical Foundations: Love Without Expectation

The Bible is filled with examples of one-way relationships — relationships built on unconditional love, selfless giving, and grace. These stories and teachings reveal a love that flows freely, without any guarantee of reciprocity, and they challenge us to rise above the natural human instinct to expect something in return. Jesus' teachings and life exemplify this radical love, providing the ultimate model for one-way relationships.

Luke 6:35: Loving Without Expecting

One of the first verses I encountered that challenged my cultural assumptions was Luke 6:35: *"But love your enemies, do good to them, and lend to them without expecting to get anything back."* This scripture introduced me to a kind of love that wasn't transactional. It wasn't about keeping score or ensuring fairness. It was about giving freely, as an act of faith, reflecting the boundless love of God.

This verse is a call to love beyond our comfort zones. It challenges us to love not just those who are easy to love but even those who may oppose us or never acknowledge our kindness. It's a love that mirrors God's grace — unearned, unconditional, and freely given. Jesus sets the standard high, calling us to reflect the love of God, who *"is kind to the ungrateful and wicked."*

In my own life, this teaching tested my faith and resolve. When I first encountered people who took my kindness for granted, my initial reaction was frustration. I wanted acknowledgment, gratitude, and fairness. But this verse taught me that the act of giving is its own reward. When we love without expecting anything in return, we align ourselves with the heart of God and experience the joy of reflecting His nature.

The Parable of the Good Samaritan

The Parable of the Good Samaritan (Luke 10:25–37) offers another profound example of one-way love. In this story, Jesus tells of a man who is beaten, robbed, and left for dead. A priest and a Levite — individuals expected to show compassion — pass him by. It is a Samaritan, someone from a group despised by the Jews, who stops to help. The Samaritan not only tends to the injured man's wounds but also takes him to an inn and pays for his care, with no expectation of repayment or recognition.

The Samaritan's actions exemplify a love that transcends cultural and social boundaries. He doesn't ask if the man will repay him or even if he deserves help. Instead, his compassion flows freely, driven by a deep sense of mercy and grace. Jesus uses this parable to redefine what it means to *"love your neighbor."* It is not about obligation or reciprocity but about seeing others through the eyes of God and extending love to them simply because they are His creation.

Jesus' Teachings on Radical Love

Jesus consistently taught and modeled a love that defied human expectations. In the Sermon on the Mount, He said, *"If anyone forces you to go one mile, go with them two miles"* (Matthew 5:41). This teaching, rooted in Roman practices of conscription, encouraged His followers to go beyond what was required or expected. It was a call to freely give more than what was demanded, not out of obligation but as an act of grace.

Another powerful teaching is found in Matthew 5:44: *"Love your enemies and pray for those who persecute you."* This command flips the natural human instinct for retaliation. Instead of seeking revenge or even fairness, Jesus calls us to extend love to those who oppose us. This kind of love is not based on the worthiness of the recipient but on the boundless love of God.

The Life of Jesus: The Ultimate One-Way Relationship

Jesus's own life is the ultimate example of one-way love. He healed the sick, fed the hungry, and forgave sinners, often without any gratitude or acknowledgment in return. On the cross, He demonstrated the greatest act of love, sacrificing Himself for humanity, knowing that many would reject His gift.

One of the most striking moments of one-way love in Jesus' life is His prayer on the cross: *"Father, forgive them, for they do not know what they are doing"* (Luke 23:34). Even in His suffering, He interceded for those who crucified Him, extending grace to those who showed Him hatred. His love was not contingent on their repentance or gratitude; it was freely given.

This kind of love is challenging to comprehend and even harder to practice. But Jesus invites us to follow His example, not relying on our own strength but on the grace that flows from Him.

Theological Basis for One-Way Love

The concept of one-way love is deeply rooted in the character of God. In Ephesians 2:8-9, Paul writes: *"For it is by grace you have been saved, through faith — and this is not from yourselves, it is the gift of God — not by works, so that no one can boast."* Grace is the cornerstone of Christian faith. It is unearned, undeserved, and freely given, and it calls us to love others in the same way.

In 1 John 4:19, we are reminded, *"We love because He first loved us."* Our capacity to love unconditionally comes from experiencing God's love for us. When we understand that we are loved not because of what we've done but because of who God is, we are freed to love others without keeping score or expecting anything in return.

Applying Biblical Foundations in Our Lives

The Bible doesn't just teach one-way love as an abstract concept; it calls us to embody it in our daily lives. Whether it's helping a neighbor, forgiving someone who has wronged us, or showing kindness to a stranger, we are invited to reflect God's grace in tangible ways. This kind of love is transformative, both for the giver and the recipient. It breaks down barriers, heals wounds, and reveals the heart of God to the world.

Living out one-way love isn't easy. It requires faith, humility, and a willingness to let go of our need for recognition or reciprocity. But as we practice this kind of love, we discover the freedom and joy that come from aligning our lives with God's grace.

Chapter 3: Personal Journey

Learning to embrace one-way relationships has been one of the most transformative journeys of my life. Through personal experiences, I came to understand that giving freely without expectation is not only a reflection of God's grace but also a source of profound joy and emotional protection. The shift from transactional relationships to one-way relationships wasn't easy, but it opened the door to a life filled with peace and purpose. In this chapter, I reflect on three pivotal moments that helped me understand the benefits of one-way relationships and how they guard the giver from resentment and burnout.

Story 1: The Dentist's Kindness — Love Without Familiarity

One of my earliest lessons in unconditional kindness came from an unexpected place: my dentist's office. During my second visit, I was greeted warmly by the receptionist and the dentist. They called me by name and asked about my son, remembering details from our previous conversation. I was touched by their apparent care but later realized they had likely read notes from my file. At first, I felt foolish, thinking their kindness was merely professional politeness rather than genuine memory.

However, as I reflected, I realized their care was no less authentic simply because it was rooted in a system. They had chosen to treat every patient with warmth and respect, regardless of how well they knew them personally. This was a striking contrast to my cultural upbringing, where relationships are built over time and care is reserved for those within one's close circle. Yet here was an example of kindness extended freely, without the expectation of deeper connection or repayment.

This "indifferentiable love," as I later came to call it, challenged my understanding of relationships. It showed me that sincere care doesn't have to be earned; it can be given as a choice, a reflection of one's character. The dentist and receptionist protected themselves from burnout by maintaining professional boundaries while still showing genuine kindness. This balance between warmth and detachment allowed them to give freely without feeling drained, a principle that would later guide my own approach to relationships.

Story 2: Paul's Love for All Children — A Lesson in Abundance

Another defining moment came during a trip to Great Wolf Lodge when I was dating Paul, my current husband. Paul took my son David and a few other children, including a much younger girl named Anna, to enjoy the water park. While David and his friends played, Paul spent most of his time caring for Anna. Initially, I felt hurt. I had hoped this trip would be an opportunity for Paul to bond with David.

But later, as I reflected on the day, I realized something important about Paul: his love wasn't selective. He treated all children with the same affection and care, not because he had to, but because that was simply who he was. The very reason Paul could love David as his own was because of that same boundless love. He didn't divide his attention; he shared it freely with everyone. That moment taught me a valuable lesson in understanding Paul's character — there was no favoritism in his heart. I shouldn't have felt hurt by his attention toward Anna because it was simply his nature to give. Watching him love unconditionally made me realize that this was the kind of love Jesus called us to show.

The Benefits of One-Way Relationships

These stories taught me that one-way relationships are not just an ideal; they are a safeguard for the giver. When we give freely, without expecting anything in return, we shield ourselves from disappointment and resentment. This mindset transforms giving from a burden into a source of joy and fulfillment.

Emotional Freedom: Letting go of expectations allows us to give without fear of rejection or ingratitude.

Sustainable Generosity: By focusing on the act of giving itself, we can continue to serve others without becoming emotionally drained.

Deeper Joy: True joy comes not from being acknowledged but from reflecting God's grace through our actions.

Liberation to Love Strangers: One-way relationships free us to love people we don't know deeply, just as the dentist's office showed me. This form of love transcends familiarity, enabling us to care for strangers in meaningful ways without needing personal ties.

One-way relationships align us with the love Jesus exemplified. They liberate us from the constraints of reciprocity and invite us to give from a place of abundance. As I have learned through these moments, the greatest benefit of one-way relationships is the freedom to love unconditionally, knowing that our reward is not in the response of others but in the peace and joy that come from reflecting God's love.

Part II: The Challenges of Loving Unconditionally

Chapter 4: When Love Is Misunderstood

Unconditional love, as beautiful and transformative as it is, does not always meet with understanding or appreciation. When we give freely without expecting anything in return, our intentions can sometimes be misinterpreted or taken for granted. These misunderstandings can lead to hurt feelings, frustration, or even emotional burnout. However, by grounding ourselves in faith, we can navigate these challenges and find strength to persevere.

The Risk of Misinterpretation

Unconditional love is often countercultural, making it difficult for others to understand or accept. In some cases, the recipient of unconditional love may feel uneasy or suspicious. They might question the giver's motives, wondering if there are hidden expectations or strings attached. This reaction is especially common in cultures or communities where relationships are traditionally reciprocal.

For example, when I offered $50 to an old girlfriend from college who needed to purchase a book for school, but was short on cash,, all she wanted to know was how soon she needed to pay it back. Her reaction reflected the deeply ingrained cultural expectation that every gift or act of kindness requires immediate repayment. While my intention was simply to help my friend, her concern about reciprocity revealed how foreign the idea of one-way giving was. Her hesitation wasn't a rejection of my gesture but a reflection of the cultural framework she operated within.

Similarly, acts of unconditional love can sometimes be perceived as patronizing or insincere. When someone offers help without expecting anything in return, the recipient might feel indebted or even resentful, mistaking generosity for pity. These misunderstandings highlight the delicate balance required in practicing one-way relationships — a balance that depends on faith and humility to sustain.

The Toll of Being Taken for Granted

Perhaps the greatest challenge in unconditional giving is the risk of being taken for granted. When love and kindness are given freely, they are not always met with gratitude. Instead, they may be overlooked or even exploited. This can be particularly painful when it involves people we care about deeply.

One of the starkest contrasts between transactional and one-way relationships became clear during my time in Pittsburgh. A family from our Chinese church hosted weekly Bible studies, opening their home to students and providing snacks and guidance. Many of the attendees weren't Christians and often took the family's generosity for granted. They would arrive without much thought for the effort it took to prepare and rarely expressed gratitude. Over time, the host family grew weary and eventually stopped hosting. Their emotional exhaustion was palpable; they felt unappreciated, their efforts unnoticed.

In contrast, I thought of Sam and Sara, a missionary couple I had known in Evanston, Illinois. For decades, they hosted Bible studies in their home, serving countless students who often lost contact after graduating. Yet, Sam and Sara never wavered in their commitment. When I asked Sara how they managed to keep going, she simply smiled and said they were planting seeds. They didn't expect to see the fruits of their labor or receive thanks from those they helped. Their joy came from knowing they were fulfilling God's calling, not from receiving acknowledgment.

The difference between these two families lay in their mindset. The host family in Pittsburgh viewed their generosity as a reciprocal act; when gratitude was absent, their emotional reserves were drained. Sam and Sara, on the other hand, embodied the spirit of one-way relationships. They gave freely, finding joy and peace in the act of giving itself. By aligning their actions with God's grace, they were protected from the hurt and burnout that come from unmet expectations.

The contrast between this family and Sam and Sara, the missionary couple I knew in Evanston, was striking. Sam and Sara hosted Bible studies for decades, knowing that most of the students they helped would never keep in touch. Yet, they never stopped giving. Their ability to persevere came from their faith. They didn't give out of a need for acknowledgment or reciprocity; they gave as an act of obedience to God and as a reflection of His grace.

The Emotional Toll of Misunderstood Love

When our love is misunderstood or unappreciated, it's natural to feel hurt or frustrated. These emotions can lead to resentment, making it difficult to continue giving. However, it's important to remember that unconditional love is not about the recipient's response; it's about the character and faith of the giver.

During my early years as a Christian, I often struggled with feelings of disappointment when my efforts to help others went unnoticed. I found myself questioning whether my actions were worthwhile if they weren't appreciated. Over time, I realized that this mindset was rooted in my own expectations, not in the principles of grace and one-way relationships. Letting go of these expectations was a difficult but necessary step in learning to love unconditionally. Faith played a pivotal role in helping me persevere. Scripture reminded me that true love isn't transactional. In 1 Corinthians 13:4-5, Paul writes, *"Love is patient, love is kind. It does not envy, it does not boast, it is not proud. It does not dishonor others, it is not self-seeking, it is not easily angered, it keeps no record of wrongs."* This passage became a guiding light for me, helping me to focus on the act of giving itself rather than the response it elicited.

Persevering Through Faith

Faith gives us the strength to continue loving even when our love is misunderstood or taken for granted. It reminds us that our ultimate reward is not found in the acknowledgment of others but in the knowledge that we are fulfilling God's will. When we ground our actions in faith, we can find peace and purpose even in the face of disappointment.

Seeing Through God's Eyes: Faith allows us to see the bigger picture, understanding that our acts of love may plant seeds that will bear fruit in ways we may never witness. Sam and Sara's story is a testament to this truth. Their joy came from knowing they were part of God's plan, not from receiving thanks or recognition.

Relying on God's Strength: Loving unconditionally requires more than human effort; it requires divine strength. When our own reserves are depleted, we can turn to God for renewal. Isaiah 40:31 reminds us, *"But those who hope in the Lord will renew their strength. They will soar on wings like eagles; they will run and not grow weary, they will walk and not be faint."*

Focusing on God's Example: Jesus Himself experienced the pain of being misunderstood and unappreciated. Yet, He continued to love without reservation, even praying for those who crucified Him. His example reminds us that the power of unconditional love lies not in its reception but in its reflection of God's grace.

Finding Freedom in Misunderstood Love

While loving unconditionally can be challenging, it also brings a profound sense of freedom. When we let go of the need for recognition, we free ourselves from the emotional weight of disappointment. This freedom allows us to love more deeply, more joyfully, and more faithfully.

Through faith, we can persevere in one-way relationships, trusting that our love reflects God's heart. Even when misunderstood, unconditional love has the power to transform both the giver and the recipient. It teaches us to rely on God's grace, to see beyond immediate outcomes, and to find joy in the simple act of giving.

Chapter 5: Protecting Yourself While Giving Freely

Practicing one-way love is a profound act of faith, but it can also leave us vulnerable to emotional exhaustion, resentment, or even manipulation if we are not careful. Giving freely doesn't mean neglecting our own needs or allowing others to take advantage of our kindness. Instead, it requires wisdom and boundaries that preserve our emotional and spiritual health without compromising the essence of unconditional love. In this chapter, we'll explore how to set these boundaries while continuing to give freely and joyfully.

The Balance Between Sacrifice and Self-Care

One-way love often calls for sacrifice, but it doesn't demand self-neglect. Just as Jesus withdrew from the crowds to pray and recharge, we too must recognize our own limitations and make space for rest and renewal. Boundaries are not barriers to love; they are safeguards that allow us to give sustainably.

Unconditional love doesn't mean saying "yes" to every request or depleting ourselves to the point of burnout. Instead, it means giving from a place of abundance, not exhaustion. To do this, we must learn to discern when and how to give. Setting healthy boundaries is an act of stewardship — caring for the resources God has entrusted to us, including our own time, energy, and emotional well-being.

Recognizing the Signs of Burnout

The emotional toll of giving without boundaries can manifest in various ways, including:

Resentment: Feeling unappreciated or exploited when your efforts go unnoticed or unreciprocated.

Exhaustion: Physical and emotional fatigue from overextending yourself.

Bitterness: Harboring negative feelings toward those you've helped.

Loss of Joy: Finding that acts of kindness feel more like obligations than blessings.

Recognizing these signs is the first step in protecting yourself. If you find yourself experiencing any of these emotions, it's a signal to reevaluate your approach and establish healthier boundaries.

Setting Boundaries While Loving Freely

1. Define Your Limits

- Be honest with yourself about your capacity. How much time, energy, or resources can you realistically give without compromising your well-being?
- Remember that limits are not a failure to love; they are an acknowledgment of your humanity.

2. Prioritize Prayer and Reflection

- Seek God's guidance in deciding when and how to give. Prayer allows us to align our actions with His will, ensuring that our giving is purposeful and Spirit-led.
- Reflect regularly on your motives. Are you giving out of love or obligation? Are you seeking approval or genuinely reflecting God's grace?
- **Learn to Say "No" Gracefully**
    - Saying "no" doesn't make you unloving. It's an essential part of maintaining balance and ensuring that your "yes" comes from a place of willingness, not compulsion.
    - Practice kind but firm responses, such as: "I wish I could help, but I don't have the capacity right now."

- **Focus on Quality, Not Quantity**
  - o One act of genuine love can have a greater impact than multiple acts done out of duty. Be intentional about the ways you give, focusing on depth rather than breadth.
- **Entrust the Outcome to God**
  - o Once you've given, release any expectations about the results. Trust that God will use your efforts for His purposes, even if you don't see the immediate impact.

The Role of Community in Supporting Givers

While one-way relationships are often personal, they don't have to be solitary. Surrounding yourself with a supportive community can provide encouragement and accountability. Share your struggles and victories with trusted friends, mentors, or small groups who understand the challenges of loving unconditionally.

In Pittsburgh, the host family who burned out from hosting Bible studies might have benefited from sharing the burden with others. Delegating tasks or rotating hosting responsibilities could have helped them sustain their generosity without feeling overwhelmed. Community not only lightens the load but also multiplies the joy of giving.

Practical Steps for Emotional and Spiritual Renewal

1. Create Space for Rest

- Schedule regular time for rest and renewal, whether through prayer, reading scripture, or simply enjoying moments of quiet.
- Follow Jesus's example of withdrawing to solitary places to pray and recharge (Luke 5:16).

2. Celebrate Small Wins

- Acknowledge the joy of giving, even in small ways. Reflect on the impact of your actions, trusting that God is at work.

3. Seek God's Strength

- When you feel depleted, turn to God for renewal. Isaiah 40:31 reminds us, *"But those who hope in the Lord will renew their strength. They will soar on wings like eagles; they will run and not grow weary, they will walk and not be faint."*

4. Practice Gratitude

- Cultivate a heart of gratitude for the opportunity to give, rather than focusing on what is received in return. Gratitude shifts our perspective from scarcity to abundance.

The Freedom Found in Boundaries

Healthy boundaries do more than protect the giver; they enhance the act of giving. By ensuring that your love flows from a place of abundance, you create space for joy, peace, and sustainability in your relationships. Boundaries free you to give without resentment, to serve without burnout, and to love without fear.

Ultimately, one-way relationships are not about how much you give but about how you give. When we set boundaries that honor both our limitations and God's calling, we protect our ability to give freely and faithfully. In doing so, we reflect the boundless love of Christ, who calls us to love not out of obligation but out of the overflow of His grace.

Chapter 6: Overcoming Cultural and Personal Expectations

The call to give without expectation often puts us at odds with societal norms and personal instincts. Many cultures, including my own Chinese heritage, emphasize reciprocity and balance in relationships. The idea of unconditional giving can be seen as strange or even naive, prompting criticism or confusion from those around us. Navigating this tension requires both conviction and wisdom, as we balance the expectations of others with our calling to reflect God's grace.

The Weight of Cultural Norms

In Chinese culture, relationships are governed by an unspoken ledger of favors and obligations. Giving is rarely a one-way act; it is part of an intricate system of reciprocity that ensures mutual benefit and harmony. While this system fosters strong networks and accountability, it can also create pressure. Failing to reciprocate can lead to feelings of shame or resentment, and giving without expectation can be viewed as foolish or even suspicious.

When I offered the gift to my fellow student, Henry, his immediate response was to ask how he could repay me. While his reaction was rooted in cultural norms, it highlighted the tension I faced as I sought to practice one-way relationships. To him, my unconditional gift seemed out of place. His response reminded me how deeply ingrained cultural expectations can be and how challenging it is to break free from them.

Similarly, personal expectations often echo these cultural norms. We naturally crave acknowledgment and fairness, making it difficult to give freely. The desire for reciprocity is deeply human, and overcoming it requires intentional effort and faith.

The Call to Radical Giving

Jesus's teachings challenge us to rise above societal norms and personal instincts. In Matthew 5:46-47, He says, *"If you love those who love you, what reward will you get? Are not even the tax collectors doing that? And if you greet only your own people, what are you doing more than others?"* This call to love beyond the boundaries of cultural expectations is at the heart of one-way relationships.

Radical giving is not about ignoring cultural norms but about transcending them. It invites us to engage with the world differently, offering love and kindness as a reflection of God's grace rather than as a response to societal pressures. This mindset doesn't reject cultural values outright; instead, it redefines them in light of God's unconditional love.

Navigating Criticism and Confusion

When you choose to practice one-way relationships, you may face criticism or confusion from others. Some may question your motives, while others may misunderstand your intentions. Here are strategies to navigate these challenges:

1. Stay Grounded in Your Purpose

Remind yourself why you are giving. Your acts of love are not about seeking approval but about reflecting God's grace. Keeping this purpose at the forefront will help you stay resilient in the face of criticism.

2. Communicate Clearly

When appropriate, explain your perspective to others. Sharing the principles of one-way relationships and the joy they bring can help others understand your actions, even if they don't fully agree.

3. Embrace Grace for Yourself and Others

Understand that not everyone will share your mindset, and that's okay. Extend grace to those who misunderstand or critique your choices, recognizing that their perspective is shaped by their own experiences and cultural norms.

4. Find Strength in Community

Surround yourself with people who share your values. A supportive community can provide encouragement and affirmation as you navigate the challenges of practicing unconditional love.

Breaking Free from Personal Expectations

Overcoming cultural norms is only part of the challenge; we must also confront our own expectations. Even when we strive to give unconditionally, our human nature often clings to the hope of recognition or reciprocation. Letting go of these expectations requires humility and trust in God.

1. Shift Your Focus

Instead of focusing on the recipient's response, focus on the act of giving itself. Celebrate the opportunity to reflect God's love, regardless of the outcome.

2. Trust God's Plan

Recognize that your efforts may have an impact beyond what you can see. Trust that God will use your acts of love in His own time and way.

3. Cultivate Gratitude

Practice gratitude for the opportunity to give, rather than for how your giving is received. Gratitude helps shift your perspective from scarcity to abundance.

Redefining Success

One of the most liberating aspects of practicing one-way relationships is redefining what it means to succeed. In a transactional world, success is often measured by results: Did the recipient appreciate my gift? Did they return the favor? In a one-way relationship, success is measured by faithfulness: Did I give with a loving heart? Did I reflect God's grace?

This shift in perspective frees us from the weight of others' expectations. It allows us to give with joy and confidence, knowing that our worth is not tied to how our love is received but to the act of giving itself.

Overcoming Cultural and Personal Expectations Through Faith

Ultimately, the strength to overcome cultural and personal expectations comes from faith. By grounding ourselves in God's love, we can rise above societal pressures and personal instincts, finding freedom and joy in giving without expectation. Scripture reminds us that our reward is not in human recognition but in fulfilling God's calling. As Galatians 6:9 encourages us, *"Let us not become weary in doing good, for at the proper time we will reap a harvest if we do not give up."*

Through faith, we can embrace the radical love of one-way relationships, navigating the challenges with grace and wisdom. As we do, we become vessels of God's grace, shining His light in a world bound by expectations.

Part III: The Joy and Power of Giving

Chapter 7: The Rewards of One-Way Relationships

Practicing one-way relationships is not without its challenges, but the rewards are immeasurable. While the world often measures success by what we receive, the act of giving itself carries profound spiritual and emotional blessings. These rewards are not contingent on the recipient's response; they flow from the freedom, peace, and joy that come from aligning our lives with God's grace. In this chapter, we'll explore the spiritual and emotional benefits for the giver and share real-life examples of how one-way relationships have blessed others.

The Spiritual Benefits of One-Way Relationships

1. Deepened Connection with God

- One-way relationships mirror God's unconditional love for us. When we give freely, we draw closer to Him, reflecting His nature and deepening our spiritual connection.
- As Jesus said in Acts 20:35, *"It is more blessed to give than to receive."* This blessing comes not

from material gain but from the joy of living out God's love.

2. A Heart Transformed by Grace

• Giving without expectation reshapes our hearts, replacing selfishness with generosity and pride with humility. It aligns us with the example of Christ, who gave His life for us without demanding anything in return.

3. Strengthened Faith

One-way relationships require trust in God's plan. When we give without guarantees, we exercise faith, believing that God will use our efforts for His purposes.

The Emotional Benefits of One-Way Relationships

1. Peace

• Letting go of expectations brings peace. We are no longer weighed down by disappointment or resentment when our love is unreciprocated.
• This peace comes from knowing that our worth is not tied to others' responses but to the act of giving itself.

2. Joy

- True joy comes not from being acknowledged but from the simple act of giving. Whether it's a kind word, a selfless act, or a gift, the process of giving fills our hearts with happiness.
- Research has even shown that acts of generosity release endorphins, creating what some call the "helper's high."

3. Resilience

- Practicing one-way relationships builds emotional resilience. By giving freely, we learn to navigate life's ups and downs with grace, finding strength in God's love rather than in external validation.

Real-Life Examples of Blessings Through One-Way Relationships

1. The Joy of Hosting Without Expectations

Sam and Sara, the missionary couple from Evanston, hosted Bible studies for decades, knowing that most of the students they helped would never keep in touch. Despite this, they found joy in the act of giving itself. They saw their home as a vessel for God's work, and their faith sustained them. Their resilience and peace came from trusting that the seeds they planted would grow, even if they never saw the harvest.

2. The Freedom to Love Strangers

The dentist and receptionist who greeted me so warmly demonstrated the power of love for strangers. They didn't know me personally, yet they chose to care for me as a patient. This seemingly small act of kindness carried a profound impact, reminding me that love doesn't have to be earned. Their approach to care created an atmosphere of peace and acceptance, benefiting not only the recipient but also the giver, who found fulfillment in their work.

3. A Family Transformed by Unconditional Love

Paul's abundant love for children, whether his own or others, reflected the resilience that comes from giving freely. His ability to care for Anna at the water park without favoritism or expectation showed me the strength and joy that flow from an overflowing heart. His actions were not motivated by duty but by the freedom to love generously, a freedom that blessed everyone involved.

4. Finding Joy in Community Service

At a local food pantry I volunteered with, I met individuals who devoted countless hours to serving others, often without recognition. One volunteer shared how her work gave her a sense of purpose and peace, knowing she was making a difference. "It's not about whether they say thank you," she said. "It's about knowing I'm doing what God called me to do." Her resilience and joy were evident, and her example inspired others to serve with the same selflessness.

The Ripple Effect of One-Way Relationships

The blessings of one-way relationships don't end with the giver. They create a ripple effect, inspiring others to give and fostering a culture of grace. When we practice one-way relationships, we become living examples of God's love, planting seeds that may grow in ways we can't predict.

1. Henry's Bible

When I gave Henry the bilingual Bible and encouraged him to "pay it forward," I had no way of knowing how that gift might impact his life or the lives of others he might bless. But I trusted that God would use it for His glory, and that trust brought me peace.

2. The Students at Sam and Sara's Home

Decades of hosting Bible studies left a legacy that touched countless lives. Even if many students didn't stay in touch, the seeds planted during those gatherings continued to bear fruit long after they left.

The Ultimate Reward

The ultimate reward of one-way relationships is the knowledge that we are fulfilling God's will. While we may not see the immediate results of our giving, we can rest in the assurance that our acts of love are part of a greater plan. As Matthew 6:20 reminds us, *"Store up for yourselves treasures in heaven, where moths and vermin do not destroy, and where thieves do not break in and steal."*

By giving freely, we align our lives with the example of Christ, finding peace, joy, and resilience along the way. These rewards are not fleeting; they are eternal, rooted in the unshakable foundation of God's love.

Chapter 8: God's Grace in Action

Practicing one-way relationships is not merely a matter of personal fulfillment; it is an act of living out God's grace. Grace is at the heart of the Christian faith — a gift freely given by God, undeserved and unconditional. When we extend one-way love to others, we reflect this divine grace, allowing it to flow through us and into the lives of those we touch. In this chapter, we'll explore how practicing one-way relationships aligns with God's grace and share stories of transformation that demonstrate the power of grace in action.

Grace: The Foundation of One-Way Relationships

Grace is what distinguishes one-way relationships from transactional ones. It is the essence of God's love for humanity, offered without regard to our worthiness or ability to repay. As Ephesians 2:8-9 reminds us, *"For it is by grace you have been saved, through faith — and this is not from yourselves, it is the gift of God — not by works, so that no one can boast."*

When we practice one-way relationships, we align ourselves with this grace. We give not because of what the recipient has done or can offer in return but because we are called to love as God loves us. This act of grace transforms both the giver and the recipient, creating a ripple effect that extends far beyond the immediate relationship.

Reflecting God's Grace in One-Way Relationships

1. Unconditional Giving

God's grace is a model for unconditional giving. Just as He gives us salvation without asking for anything in return, we are called to extend love, kindness, and generosity without expectation. This kind of giving reflects the heart of God and draws us closer to Him.

2. Extending Forgiveness

One-way relationships often require us to forgive others who may have hurt us or taken us for granted without remorse or repentance. This forgiveness is an expression of grace, allowing us to let go of resentment and love freely. As Colossians 3:13 instructs, *"Forgive as the Lord forgave you."*

3. Trusting in God's Plan

Practicing one-way relationships means trusting that God will use our efforts for His purposes, even if we don't see immediate results. It requires faith that our acts of love and grace will bear fruit in ways we may never witness.

Stories of Transformation

1. The Chain of Generosity

When I gave my classmate the money she needed to buy her book, and encouraged her to "pay it forward," I had no way of knowing how that act of grace would impact her life. While I didn't expect anything in return, the possibility that she might one day pass on the gift of faith to someone else brought me joy. This simple act of one-way love reflected God's grace and reminded me that even small gestures can have a profound impact.

2. The Missionaries Who Planted Seeds

Sam and Sara, the missionary couple who hosted Bible studies in Evanston, exemplified God's grace in action. They gave freely, opening their home to countless students over the years, many of whom never stayed in touch. Yet, their joy and resilience came from knowing they were planting seeds of faith. Their commitment inspired transformation not only in the lives of the students they served but also in the communities those students eventually touched.

3. A Stranger's Grace at a Food Pantry

During a visit to a local food pantry, I met a volunteer named Mary, who shared her story of transformation. She had once been a recipient of the pantry's services, struggling to provide for her family. Over time, she found stability and began volunteering at the same pantry. Her decision to give back was an expression of gratitude, but it was also a reflection of God's grace at work in her life. Mary's story reminded me that grace doesn't stop with the recipient; it continues to flow, inspiring others to give.

4. My Transformation as a Giver

Early in my journey, I often gave with subtle expectations, hoping for acknowledgment or reciprocation. As I grew in my faith, I learned to let go of these desires, finding freedom in unconditional giving. Hosting Bible studies at our house, helping others, or simply showing kindness without expecting anything in return brought me a sense of peace and purpose. This transformation allowed me to experience the joy of living out God's grace.

The Power of Grace to Transform Lives

God's grace has the power to transform not only individuals but also relationships and communities. When we practice one-way relationships, we become conduits of His grace, allowing it to flow into the lives of those around us. This transformation often occurs in unexpected ways:

1. Healing Relationships

Acts of unconditional love can heal broken relationships, offering forgiveness and restoration where resentment once thrived.

2. Inspiring Generosity

One act of grace can inspire others to give, creating a chain of generosity that impacts countless lives.

3. Building Faith

When others witness the grace we extend, they may be drawn to the source of that grace — God Himself.

Aligning Our Lives with God's Grace

Practicing one-way relationships is a way of aligning our lives with God's purposes. It invites us to participate in His redemptive work, bringing love and hope to a world in need. As 1 Peter 4:10 reminds us, *"Each of you should use whatever gift you have received to serve others, as faithful stewards of God's grace in its various forms."*

When we give freely, forgive generously, and love unconditionally, we become living examples of God's grace. This alignment not only transforms our own hearts but also allows us to be vessels of His love, bringing light to those around us.

Living Out God's Grace

Living out God's grace through one-way relationships is not always easy, but it is profoundly rewarding. It challenges us to rise above cultural norms and personal expectations, finding freedom in the act of giving itself. As we reflect His grace, we experience its transformative power in our own lives and witness its impact on others.

Through stories of transformation — mine and others' — I've come to see that practicing one-way relationships is more than an act of kindness; it is a way of embodying God's grace. It reminds us that we are not the source of this love but its stewards, called to share it freely with the world.

Part IV: Practicing One-Way Relationships

Chapter 9: In the Family: Loving Children, Spouses, and Stepchildren

Family is often where the most profound lessons in love and grace are learned. Practicing one-way relationships within the family can strengthen bonds, foster emotional resilience, and create an atmosphere of unconditional acceptance. However, it also challenges us to confront cultural norms, personal expectations, and our own limitations. In this chapter, we'll explore how one-way relationships can transform family dynamics, with a focus on parenting, step-parenting, and adoption. By examining cultural contrasts and personal stories, we'll uncover the beauty and power of loving without expectation.

The Transformative Power of One-Way Love in Family

Family relationships are often the most emotionally charged and complex. Whether it's the unconditional love of a parent, the selflessness of a spouse, or the unique challenges of blended families, one-way relationships provide a foundation for growth and connection.

1. Strengthening Bonds Through Unconditional Love

- One-way relationships create a safe space where family members can thrive without fear of judgment or rejection. When love is given freely, it fosters trust and deepens emotional intimacy.
- For example, when Paul cared for Anna, the young girl we brought to Great Wolf Lodge, his selfless attention showed me the transformative power of one-way love. He didn't prioritize her because she was more deserving; he loved her because that's who he was. That same abundant love allowed him to bond deeply with my son, David, as a stepfather.

2. Freedom from Expectations

- Practicing one-way love in family life frees us from the burden of unmet expectations. Instead of measuring relationships by what we receive, we find joy in the act of giving itself.
- This mindset was evident in Paul's ability to treat all children equally, whether they were biologically his or not. His love wasn't based on obligation or reciprocity but on an overflow of grace.

Cultural Contrasts in Parenting

Parenting practices often reflect cultural norms, which can shape how love is given and received within families. The contrast between Chinese and American approaches to parenting reveals the profound impact of grace and unconditional love.

1. Conditional Love in Chinese Culture

- In traditional Chinese culture, parenting often emphasizes achievement and reciprocity. Children are expected to bring honor to the family through academic success and filial piety, and parents may feel their love is contingent on these outcomes.
- This conditional approach can create pressure and strain within the family. Children may feel that their worth is tied to their accomplishments, while parents may struggle with disappointment if expectations aren't met.

2. Unconditional Love in American Culture

- Many American families, especially those influenced by Christian values, embrace a more unconditional approach to parenting. They view children as gifts from God, deserving of love regardless of their achievements or abilities.

- This perspective is particularly evident in the adoption of children with disabilities. American families often see these adoptions as a calling, an opportunity to reflect God's grace and provide a loving home for children who may otherwise be overlooked.

Step-Parenting and Blended Families

Blending families introduces unique challenges, as step-parents and stepchildren navigate new roles and relationships. One-way love is essential in this context, as it allows families to build trust and connection without the weight of expectations.

1. Paul's Example

- Paul's relationship with David demonstrated the power of one-way love in step-parenting. He didn't demand immediate affection or loyalty from David; instead, he focused on loving him unconditionally. Over time, this approach fostered a deep bond that was based on trust and mutual respect.

2. Loving Through Grace

- Step-parents often face resistance or indifference from stepchildren, especially in the early stages of a blended family. Practicing one-way love means giving without expecting immediate acceptance, knowing that the relationship will grow in its own time.

- This grace-filled approach creates a foundation of stability and security, allowing stepchildren to feel valued and loved without pressure.

The Grace of Adoption

Adoption is one of the most profound expressions of one-way love, as it reflects God's own adoption of us into His family. Families who adopt, particularly those who embrace children with disabilities or other challenges, exemplify the transformative power of grace.

1. American Families and Adoption

Many American families see adoption as a calling, a way to live out their faith and provide unconditional love to children in need. This contrasts with cultural norms in some societies where children with disabilities may be seen as burdens rather than blessings.

2. A Reflection of God's Love

Adoption mirrors God's grace, as it involves welcoming a child into the family without regard to their ability to repay or meet expectations. It is a powerful reminder that love is not earned but freely given.

Practical Steps for Practicing One-Way Love in Family Life

1. Focus on the Act of Giving

Celebrate the joy of loving unconditionally, rather than focusing on the response. Whether it's preparing a meal, offering encouragement, or simply being present, find fulfillment in the act itself.

2. Let Go of Expectations

Release the need for immediate results or recognition. Trust that your love is planting seeds that will grow in time.

3. Extend Grace During Conflict

Family relationships often involve misunderstandings and disagreements. Responding with grace rather than retaliation can diffuse tension and pave the way for reconciliation.

4. Model Unconditional Love

Children and spouses learn by example. When you practice one-way love, you create an environment where others feel safe to do the same.

The Reward of Loving Without Expectation

Practicing one-way relationships in the family brings countless rewards, both seen and unseen. It fosters resilience, builds trust, and creates a legacy of grace that impacts future generations. By loving unconditionally, we reflect the love of Christ and create a home where peace and joy flourish.

As I've learned through my own experiences, one-way love is not about perfection or always getting it right. It's about showing up with a heart willing to give, trusting that God will use our efforts to strengthen the bonds of family and transform our relationships into a reflection of His grace.

Chapter 10: In the Church and Community

The church and community are powerful settings for practicing one-way relationships. Rooted in the example of Christ, these spaces often embody one-way love through service, charity, and outreach. Acts of kindness performed within the church and community do not depend on the recipient's ability to repay or even express gratitude. Instead, they reflect God's grace and provide an opportunity for believers to demonstrate their faith in action. In this chapter, we'll explore how churches and community groups model one-way love and offer practical guidance for participating in or starting initiatives.

The Church as a Reflection of God's Grace

The church is called to be the hands and feet of Christ, extending His love to all people without discrimination or expectation. This mission is evident in countless ministries and initiatives that prioritize giving over receiving.

1. Acts of Service and Charity

- Many churches host food pantries, clothing drives, or shelter programs for the homeless. These efforts often serve individuals who cannot repay the kindness extended to them, reflecting the unconditional love of Christ.
- For example, the International Chinese Christian Conference (ICCC) I attended provided meals, lodging, and services free of charge. The organizers didn't expect attendees to contribute financially or offer thanks; their sole purpose was to bless others and glorify God.

2. Missionary Work

- Missionaries, like Sam and Sara in Evanston, dedicate their lives to sharing the gospel and serving communities. They often work in challenging environments, giving freely of their time and resources to plant seeds of faith. Their work exemplifies one-way love, as they serve with no guarantee of recognition or visible results.

3. Community Outreach

- Outreach programs, such as tutoring for underprivileged students or prison ministries, often involve giving to those who may never repay the favor. These efforts reflect God's grace, creating opportunities for transformation and hope.

One-Way Love in Community Groups

Beyond the church, community groups also play a vital role in practicing one-way relationships. Whether secular or faith-based, these organizations bring people together to serve others and build stronger, more compassionate communities.

1. Volunteering as a Practice of Grace

- Volunteering is a tangible way to practice one-way love. From serving meals at a soup kitchen to mentoring a child, these acts of kindness often benefit individuals who may never be able to repay the favor.
- For example, at a local food pantry where I volunteered, many of the clients didn't have the means to give back. Yet, the joy of serving them brought peace and purpose to the volunteers, demonstrating that the reward lies in the act of giving itself.

2. Building Inclusive Communities

- Community groups that focus on inclusivity, such as those supporting individuals with disabilities or immigrant families, embody one-way love by creating spaces where all are valued and supported, regardless of their background or circumstances.

Practical Guidance for Participating in or Starting Initiatives

1. Identify Your Passion

Consider the causes or groups that resonate most deeply with you. Whether it's caring for the homeless, mentoring youth, visiting the elderly, or supporting single parents, your passion can guide you to meaningful opportunities for service.

2. Start Small

If you're new to serving, begin with small, manageable commitments. Volunteer for a single event, join a short-term mission trip, or participate in a local charity drive. Small acts of love can have a big impact and help you build confidence in giving.

3. Join an Existing Ministry or Group

Many churches and community organizations have established programs that welcome new participants. Joining an existing initiative allows you to learn from experienced leaders and contribute to ongoing efforts.

4. Start Your Own Initiative

If you see a need that isn't being met, consider starting your own initiative. Begin by identifying the resources and support you'll need, then invite others to join you. For example:

- Host a Bible study for newcomers in your community.
- Organize a neighborhood cleanup day.
- Start a donation drive for a local shelter or food pantry.

5. Focus on Relationship-Building

Service is more than meeting physical needs; it's also about building relationships. Take the time to listen to and connect with those whom you serve, demonstrating one-way love through both actions and presence.

6. Involve Others

Invite friends, family, or church members to join you in serving. Collaborating with others not only increases the impact of your efforts but also creates a sense of shared purpose and joy.

Challenges in Serving

Serving others, especially in one-way relationships, is not without its challenges. Volunteers may experience burnout, frustration, or discouragement when their efforts go unrecognized or when progress seems slow. To navigate these challenges:

1. Stay Rooted in Faith

Remember that your service is an act of obedience to God, not a quest for recognition. Trust that He will use your efforts in ways you may not see.

2. Celebrate Small Wins

Focus on the positive impact you're making, even if it feels small. Each act of love contributes to a larger ripple effect.

3. Seek Support from Others

Share your struggles with trusted friends or mentors who can encourage you and pray for you.

The Rewards of Serving in the Church and Community

The rewards of serving in the church and community extend beyond personal fulfillment. They include:

1. Deepened Faith

Serving allows you to live out your faith in tangible ways, strengthening your relationship with God.

2. Stronger Connections

Serving alongside others fosters a sense of belonging and shared purpose.

3. Impact on Lives

Your efforts may inspire transformation in others, even if you don't witness the results firsthand.

Living Out One-Way Love

Practicing one-way love in the church and community is a powerful way to reflect God's grace. It challenges us to move beyond our comfort zones and give without expecting anything in return. By participating in or starting initiatives, we become part of God's work in the world, creating spaces of hope, healing, and transformation.

As we serve, we are reminded that the greatest reward is not in what we receive but in the joy of giving. Through one-way love, we not only bless others but also align ourselves with the heart of Christ, living out His command to love our neighbors as ourselves.

Chapter 11: In Everyday Life

One-way relationships don't have to be confined to grand gestures or organized initiatives. They can be practiced in the quiet moments of everyday life — in how we interact with our coworkers, neighbors, and even strangers. Unconditional love, when woven into the fabric of daily interactions, creates ripples that can transform not only others' lives but also our own. In this chapter, we'll explore practical tips for showing one-way love in day-to-day interactions and share stories of how simple acts of grace can make a lasting impact.

The Power of Small Acts of Kindness

Everyday life offers countless opportunities to practice one-way relationships. While these acts may seem small, their impact can be profound, especially when given freely and without expectation.

1. A Kind Word or Compliment

Words have the power to uplift and encourage. Compliment a coworker on their effort, thank a cashier for their service, or simply greet someone with a smile. These small gestures can brighten someone's day and show them they are valued.

2. Acts of Service

Helping others in practical ways is a tangible expression of love. Hold the door for someone, offer to carry a heavy load, or bring coffee to a colleague. These simple acts demonstrate care and thoughtfulness.

3. Listening Without Interrupting

In a fast-paced world, giving someone your undivided attention is a gift. Listen to a friend's struggles, let a coworker share their ideas, or ask your neighbor how they're doing — and truly listen.

One-Way Love at Work

The workplace is an environment often governed by performance and competition, making it an ideal setting to practice one-way relationships. By showing grace and kindness to colleagues, we can create a more positive and supportive atmosphere.

1. Celebrate Others' Success

Congratulate a coworker on their achievements, even if you feel overlooked. Celebrating others without envy fosters goodwill and strengthens relationships.

2. Offer Help Without Being Asked

If a teammate is struggling with a task, offer assistance without waiting for them to ask. This act of initiative shows that you care about their success and well-being.

3. Forgive Workplace Frustrations

When conflicts arise, choose forgiveness over resentment. Responding with grace instead of retaliation can diffuse tension and set a positive example.

One-Way Love with Strangers

Interacting with strangers provides unique opportunities to practice one-way relationships, as these moments are often fleeting and require no ongoing commitment.

1. Pay It Forward

Pay for someone's coffee or meal in line behind you, leave a generous tip, or donate to a cause anonymously. These acts of generosity are a reflection of grace, given freely and without expectation.

2. Show Patience

When dealing with customer service representatives, store clerks, or drivers on the road, practice patience and kindness, even in frustrating situations. A calm and understanding demeanor can make a difference in someone's day.

3. Offer a Helping Hand

If you see someone in need, such as an elderly person struggling with groceries or a parent managing young children, step in to help. These small actions reflect God's love in tangible ways.

The Role of Intentionality

Practicing one-way relationships in everyday life requires intentionality. It's easy to rush through the day, focused on our own needs and priorities, but pausing to show kindness and grace can turn ordinary moments into opportunities for transformation.

1. Start Each Day with a Giving Mindset

Begin your day with a prayer or affirmation, asking God to guide you in showing love to others. This sets the tone for intentional acts of kindness.

2. Look for Opportunities to Give

Train yourself to notice where help or encouragement is needed. Whether it's a coworker who looks overwhelmed or a stranger who seems downcast, be attuned to the needs around you.

3. Practice Gratitude

Cultivating gratitude helps shift your focus from what you lack to what you can give. When you recognize the blessings in your own life, you're more likely to share them with others.

Stories of Everyday Grace

1. The Stranger Who Paid for My Coffee

On a busy morning, I stopped at a coffee shop, feeling rushed and stressed. When I reached the counter, the barista told me my coffee had been paid for by the person ahead of me. That small act of kindness lifted my spirits and reminded me of the power of giving without expecting anything in return.

2. A Coworker's Encouragement

During a particularly challenging project at work, a colleague left a note on my desk that simply read, "You're doing great. Keep going!" That note took only seconds to write but had a lasting impact, giving me the encouragement I needed to persevere.

3. Helping a Mother in Need

While shopping at a grocery store, I noticed a mother struggling to keep her young children calm while managing a full cart. I offered to help her unload her groceries at the checkout, and the relief on her face was priceless. That small gesture cost me nothing but a few minutes of my time, yet it made a difference in her day.

The Rewards of Everyday One-Way Love

When we practice one-way relationships in daily life, the rewards are both immediate and long-lasting:

1. A Sense of Purpose

Giving to others, even in small ways, infuses everyday life with meaning and joy.

2. Stronger Connections

Acts of kindness foster a sense of community and goodwill, even among strangers.

3. Spiritual Growth

By showing grace in the ordinary, we align our lives with God's calling, growing in faith and compassion.

Living Grace in the Ordinary

One-way love in everyday life doesn't require extraordinary effort. It's about seeing the opportunities in front of us and choosing to respond with kindness, patience, and generosity. Whether it's a smile, a kind word, or a helping hand, these small acts of grace reflect God's love and remind us of the beauty in simple, selfless giving.

As you go about your day, remember that every interaction is an opportunity to practice one-way relationships. Through these moments, you not only bless others but also experience the joy and peace that come from living out God's grace.

Part V: Transforming the World Through Grace

Chapter 12: Building a Culture of One-Way Love

One-way love has the power to transform not only individual relationships but also entire communities and societies. When practiced collectively, it creates a culture of generosity, kindness, and grace that transcends boundaries and fosters unity. In a world often divided by cultural, social, and economic differences, one-way relationships offer a path to healing and reconciliation. This chapter explores the societal impact of embracing one-way love, particularly in multicultural settings, and highlights inspiring stories of movements and individuals who have embodied this transformative love.

The Societal Impact of One-Way Love

1. Breaking Down Barriers

- One-way relationships have the unique ability to bridge divides, whether they are cultural, racial, or socioeconomic. By giving without expectation, we communicate that all people are valued, regardless of their background or circumstances.

- In multicultural settings, one-way love fosters understanding and mutual respect. It challenges stereotypes and prejudices, creating an environment where diversity is celebrated rather than feared.

2. Creating Ripple Effects

- Acts of one-way love inspire others to give, creating a ripple effect that extends far beyond the initial act. This chain of generosity can transform communities, fostering a culture of compassion and selflessness.
- For example, a community food pantry that serves those in need without requiring proof of income or other qualifications demonstrates one-way love. Recipients often feel inspired to give back when they are able, perpetuating a cycle of kindness.

3. Healing Social Divisions

- One-way love can mend relationships between groups that have been historically divided. By prioritizing grace over grievance, communities can move toward reconciliation and unity.

One-Way Love in Multicultural Settings

In multicultural societies, one-way love takes on an even greater significance. It provides a way to navigate cultural differences and build bridges between communities.

1. Respecting Differences

- One-way love respects and values the unique traditions and perspectives of others without demanding conformity. It seeks to understand rather than judge, creating space for genuine connection.

2. Welcoming Immigrants and Refugees

- Communities that practice one-way love often take the lead in welcoming immigrants and refugees. By providing resources, friendship, and support without expecting anything in return, they help newcomers feel valued and included.
- For example, a church that offers free language classes or job training for immigrants exemplifies one-way love in action. These programs don't require participants to join the church; they are simply acts of service rooted in grace.

3. Fostering Inclusive Communities

- One-way love creates inclusive spaces where all people, regardless of their background, can feel at home. These communities prioritize relationships over transactions, fostering trust and collaboration.

Inspiring Stories of One-Way Love

1. The Story of Mother Teresa

- Mother Teresa's work with the poor and dying in Calcutta is one of the most iconic examples of one-way love. She cared for those who could offer her nothing in return, often in the most challenging circumstances. Her life was a testament to the transformative power of grace, as she gave freely and selflessly, trusting in God to sustain her efforts.

2. The Civil Rights Movement

- Leaders like Dr. Martin Luther King Jr. modeled one-way love by advocating for justice and equality through nonviolent resistance. Their commitment to loving their enemies and responding to hatred with grace had a profound impact, inspiring change not only in the United States but around the world.

3. Organizations Embracing One-Way Love

- **Habitat for Humanity**: This organization builds homes for families in need, relying on volunteers and donations. Recipients are not required to repay the kindness but are often encouraged to "pay it forward" by helping others in their communities.

- **The American Red Cross**: This global humanitarian organization provides aid to people affected by disasters, regardless of their nationality, religion, or political affiliation, exemplifying one-way love on a massive scale.

4. The Good Samaritan Fund

- A local church I once attended created a "Good Samaritan Fund" to help individuals in the community with unexpected financial hardships, such as medical bills or utility payments. The fund was distributed anonymously, and recipients were not required to repay or even acknowledge the gift. This initiative reflected God's grace, offering help without strings attached.

Building a Culture of One-Way Love

1. Start with Small Acts

Transforming a community begins with individual actions. Small acts of kindness — like mentoring a student, visiting a neighbor, or volunteering at a shelter — can create a ripple effect that inspires others.

2. Lead by Example

Leaders in churches, workplaces, and communities can model one-way love by serving others selflessly. Their actions set the tone for a culture of generosity and grace.

3. Encourage Storytelling

Sharing stories of one-way love helps spread the message and inspires others to follow suit. Create spaces where individuals can share their experiences of giving and receiving unconditional love.

4. Partner with Like-Minded Organizations

Collaborate with organizations that embody one-way love to amplify your impact. Partnerships can extend the reach of your efforts and inspire broader change.

The Transformative Power of One-Way Love

Building a culture of one-way love is not easy, but its impact is profound. It challenges societal norms, breaks down barriers, and creates spaces where grace can flourish. As individuals, families, and communities embrace this mindset, they reflect the heart of God and demonstrate the beauty of His love to the world.

As we seek to transform our communities and societies, let us remember the words of Jesus in John 13:34-35: *"A new command I give you: Love one another. As I have loved you, so you must love one another. By this everyone will know that you are my disciples, if you love one another."* Through one-way love, we not only change the world around us but also point others toward the source of all grace and love.

Chapter 13: Passing It Forward

One-way love is a gift, not meant to be hoarded but shared. When we experience the joy and peace of unconditional love, the natural response is to pass it forward, allowing its ripple effects to touch the lives of others. By cultivating one-way relationships in our own lives and communities, we participate in God's redemptive work, creating a legacy of grace that transcends our own efforts. In this final chapter, we'll reflect on the power of one-way love to inspire change and encourage readers to embrace this practice as a way of life.

The Ripple Effects of One-Way Love

1. Love That Multiplies

One-way love has a multiplying effect. When we give freely, we inspire others to do the same, creating a chain reaction of kindness and grace. A simple act of generosity can grow into something far greater than we imagined.

2. Transforming Relationships

Unconditional love has the power to heal broken relationships, build trust, and deepen connections. By choosing to love without expectation, we set an example for others, encouraging them to embrace grace in their own lives.

3. Inspiring Communities

As individuals practice one-way love, their actions can inspire entire communities to adopt a culture of generosity and compassion. This collective impact creates environments where grace flourishes and barriers are broken.

Cultivating One-Way Relationships

Passing it forward begins with intentionality. By making one-way love a daily practice, we can transform our relationships and communities. Here are some practical ways to cultivate one-way relationships:

1. Start Small

Look for small opportunities to give without expectation. Offer a compliment, lend a helping hand, or simply listen to someone who needs to talk. These small acts of kindness can have a profound impact.

2. Be Present

One of the greatest gifts we can offer is our presence. Whether it's spending time with a loved one or reaching out to someone in need, being fully present communicates care and value.

3. Teach by Example

Demonstrate one-way love in your own actions, whether at home, work, or in the community. Your example can inspire others to follow suit.

4. Encourage a "Pay It Forward" Mentality

When you give, encourage the recipient to pass it forward. This not only extends the impact of your kindness but also reinforces the value of one-way love.

Stories of Passing It Forward

1. The Chain of Bibles

The church Paul and I attend regularly frequently offer free Bibles to anyone who needs or wants one. Similar to when I gave Henry the bilingual Bible, they know this simple act of kindness will bring its recipients closer to God. Not only by bringing them closer to God's word, but also by planting a seed of generosity. We know it will inspire them to share the gift of faith with someone else, creating a ripple effect that extends well beyond our reach.

2. A Legacy of Service

Sam and Sara's decades of hosting Bible studies in their home left a legacy of one-way love. They certainly inspired me to one day begin a Bible Study in my home. The countless participants served "pays forward" their kindness and grace into their lives and communities, spreading generosity far and wide.

3. A Stranger's Kindness

At a grocery store, a woman once paid for my items when I realized I had forgotten my wallet. Her simple gesture reminded me of the power of one-way love, and it inspired me to do the same for someone else the next time I had the opportunity.

Reflecting on the Legacy of Unconditional Love

One-way relationships leave a lasting legacy, not because of what we receive but because of the lives we touch. The impact of unconditional love is often invisible, unfolding over time in ways we may never witness. Yet, the ripple effects are undeniable, creating waves of grace that spread far beyond our own efforts.

1. A Legacy That Transcends Generations

Acts of one-way love often inspire future generations to adopt the same mindset. Children raised in homes where unconditional love is practiced are more likely to carry those values into their own relationships and communities.

2. A Reflection of God's Kingdom

Each act of one-way love is a reflection of God's grace and a glimpse of His kingdom on earth. When we give without expectation, we participate in His work of redemption and renewal.

3. An Eternal Impact

The legacy of one-way love extends beyond this life. As we live out God's grace, we store up treasures in heaven and contribute to His eternal plan.

A Call to Action

As we conclude this journey, I invite you to embrace one-way relationships as a way of life. Let your love be a reflection of God's grace, given freely and without expectation. Start small, be intentional, and trust that your acts of kindness will create ripples that transform lives.

Remember the words of Jesus in Matthew 5:16: *"Let your light shine before others, that they may see your good deeds and glorify your Father in heaven."* By passing it forward, you not only bless others but also glorify God, leaving a legacy of love that will endure for generations.

Conclusion: A Life of Abundance

The journey of embracing one-way relationships is one of the most liberating and transformative paths we can take. It challenges societal norms, reshapes our understanding of love, and aligns us with the heart of God. By giving freely without expecting anything in return, we experience a life of abundance — one filled with joy, peace, and purpose.

In a world often consumed by transactional relationships and conditional love, one-way relationships stand out as a powerful reflection of God's grace. They remind us that love doesn't have to be earned and that true freedom comes from letting go of expectations. This shift in perspective not only transforms our own hearts but also creates a ripple effect that touches the lives of others and fosters a culture of grace and generosity.

The Freedom of One-Way Love

Practicing one-way relationships frees us from the burden of unmet expectations. It allows us to give with open hearts, finding joy in the act of giving itself rather than in how it is received. This freedom protects us from the emotional toll of resentment and burnout, creating space for peace and resilience.

One-way love also liberates us to love without limits. It empowers us to care for strangers, forgive those who have wronged us, and serve our families, churches, and communities without hesitation. In doing so, we reflect the boundless love of Christ, whose grace is freely given to us.

The Call to Practice Unconditional Love

The world is in desperate need of one-way love. In our homes, workplaces, and neighborhoods, there are countless opportunities to reflect God's grace through acts of unconditional kindness and generosity. These moments, however small, have the potential to inspire change and create lasting impact. As you step into this calling, remember that one-way love is not about perfection but about intentionality. It's about showing up with a heart willing to give and trusting that God will use your efforts in ways you may never see.

A Reflection of God's Grace

Ultimately, one-way relationships are a reflection of the grace we have received. As Ephesians 4:32 reminds us, *"Be kind and compassionate to one another, forgiving each other, just as in Christ God forgave you."* When we practice one-way love, we mirror God's forgiveness, kindness, and compassion, becoming vessels of His redemptive work in the world.

The legacy of one-way relationships is eternal. Each act of unconditional love is a seed planted in faith, capable of growing into something far greater than we could imagine. By living out this love, we participate in God's mission of renewal and bring His kingdom closer to earth.

An Inspirational Call to Action

As you close this book, I encourage you to embrace one-way love as a daily practice. Let it shape your interactions, your relationships, and your perspective on life. Start small, trust in God's guidance, and watch as His grace works through you to transform the world around you.

Remember, you are not called to love perfectly, but faithfully. Every act of one-way love, no matter how small, reflects the heart of God and contributes to His greater plan. As you live out this calling, you will discover the abundance that comes from giving freely — a life rooted in grace, filled with purpose, and overflowing with joy.

Let us go forward together, committed to practicing one-way relationships as a reflection of God's love. Through our actions, may we shine His light and inspire others to join us in creating a world transformed by grace.

Appendix

Reflection Questions: For personal journaling or group discussion.

These reflection questions are designed to help you process the concepts of one-way relationships and apply them to your own life. Use them for personal journaling, group discussions, or as prompts for deeper spiritual reflection.

Personal Journey

1. Understanding Unconditional Love

Reflect on a time when you experienced unconditional love. How did it make you feel? How did it impact your life or perspective on relationships?

2. Giving Without Expectation

Think of a situation where you gave freely without expecting anything in return. What motivated you to give, and how did it affect your heart and mindset?

3. Cultural Influence

How has your cultural background shaped your approach to relationships? What aspects of those cultural norms align with or challenge the idea of one-way love?

4. Faith in Practice

How has your faith influenced your understanding and practice of one-way relationships? In what ways has it strengthened your ability to give freely?

Challenges

1. Misunderstood Love

Have you ever felt hurt or disappointed when your love or kindness was misunderstood or taken for granted? How did you respond, and what did you learn from the experience?

2. Setting Boundaries

Reflect on a time when you felt emotionally or physically drained from giving. What boundaries could you have set to protect yourself while continuing to give freely?

3. Overcoming Expectations

Is there a relationship in your life where you struggle to let go of expectations? How might practicing one-way love transform that relationship?

Practical Application

1. Opportunities for Giving

Look around your daily life — at home, work, church, or in your community. Where do you see opportunities to practice one-way love?

2. Acts of Kindness

What are three small, intentional ways you could show unconditional love in your life this week? Who might benefit from these actions?

3. Encouraging Others

How can you inspire others in your family, workplace, or community to embrace the principles of one-way relationships?

Faith and Legacy

1. Biblical Inspiration

Which scripture about love and grace resonates most deeply with you? How can it guide your actions in practicing one-way relationships?

2. Your Legacy

If you were to look back on your life, what legacy of unconditional love would you hope to leave behind? What steps can you take now to start building that legacy?

3. Trusting God's Plan

Are there moments when you find it hard to trust that your one-way love will make a difference? How does your faith help you overcome those doubts?

These questions are an invitation to dive deeper into the practice of one-way love and to reflect on its transformative potential in your life and relationships. Use them to challenge yourself, grow in grace, and inspire others to pass it forward.

Scripture Guide: Key verses about unconditional love and grace.

These Bible verses highlight the transformative power of unconditional love and grace. Reflect on these scriptures as a source of inspiration and guidance for practicing one-way relationships in your daily life.

God's Unconditional Love

1. John 3:16

"For God so loved the world that He gave His one and only Son, that whoever believes in Him shall not perish but have eternal life."

2. Romans 5:8

"But God demonstrates His own love for us in this: While we were still sinners, Christ died for us."

3. 1 John 4:19

"We love because He first loved us."

4. Psalm 103:11-12

"For as high as the heavens are above the earth, so great is His love for those who fear Him; as far as the east is from the west, so far has He removed our transgressions from us."

The Call to Love Others Unconditionally

1. Matthew 5:44

"But I tell you, love your enemies and pray for those who persecute you."

2. Luke 6:35

"But love your enemies, do good to them, and lend to them without expecting to get anything back. Then your reward will be great, and you will be children of the Most High, because He is kind to the ungrateful and wicked."

3. 1 Corinthians 13:4-5

"Love is patient, love is kind. It does not envy, it does not boast, it is not proud. It does not dishonor others, it is not self-seeking, it is not easily angered, it keeps no record of wrongs."

4. Colossians 3:12-13

"Therefore, as God's chosen people, holy and dearly loved, clothe yourselves with compassion, kindness, humility, gentleness, and patience. Bear with each other and forgive one another if any of you has a grievance against someone. Forgive as the Lord forgave you."

Grace as a Gift

1. Ephesians 2:8-9

"For it is by grace you have been saved, through faith — and this is not from yourselves, it is the gift of God — not by works, so that no one can boast."

2. Romans 6:14

"For sin shall no longer be your master, because you are not under the law, but under grace."

3. 2 Corinthians 12:9

"But He said to me, 'My grace is sufficient for you, for My power is made perfect in weakness.' Therefore I will boast all the more gladly about my weaknesses, so that Christ's power may rest on me."

4. Titus 3:4-5

"But when the kindness and love of God our Savior appeared, He saved us, not because of righteous things we had done, but because of His mercy. He saved us through the washing of rebirth and renewal by the Holy Spirit."

The Legacy of Grace and Love

1. Matthew 5:16

"Let your light shine before others, that they may see your good deeds and glorify your Father in heaven."

2. Galatians 6:9

"Let us not become weary in doing good, for at the proper time we will reap a harvest if we do not give up."

3. 1 Peter 4:8

"Above all, love each other deeply, because love covers over a multitude of sins."

4. Matthew 6:3-4

"But when you give to the needy, do not let your left hand know what your right hand is doing, so that

your giving may be in secret. Then your Father, who sees what is done in secret, will reward you. "

These verses serve as a foundation for living out one-way love in every aspect of life. Let them guide your reflections, strengthen your faith, and inspire you to practice unconditional love as a reflection of God's grace.

Practical Exercises: Ideas for readers to practice one-way relationships in various areas of their lives.

Here are practical exercises to help you integrate one-way relationships into your daily life. These activities are designed to encourage unconditional love and grace in various areas of your life, from family and friends to your workplace and community. Start small and let these practices grow into habits that reflect God's love.

In the Family

1. Daily Acts of Kindness

Perform one small act of kindness for a family member each day, such as preparing their favorite meal, helping with chores, or leaving an encouraging note. Do it without expecting acknowledgment or gratitude.

2. Listening with Patience

Dedicate time to listen to a family member without interrupting or offering solutions. Show them they are valued simply by being present.

3. Forgive Freely

Identify a recent disagreement or hurt within your family and choose to forgive without waiting for an apology or recognition.

4. Serve Quietly

Take on a task that isn't your responsibility — clean up after dinner, fold someone's laundry, or organize a shared space — and do it anonymously.

With Friends and Neighbors

1. Send Encouragement

Write a heartfelt note, email, or text to a friend or neighbor, expressing your appreciation or offering encouragement.

2. Extend an Invitation

Invite a neighbor or acquaintance to coffee, dinner, or an event, even if they haven't reached out to you first. Use the time to deepen your relationship.

3. Surprise Generosity

Bring a small gift, such as baked goods or flowers, to a neighbor without any specific reason or occasion.

4. Help Without Being Asked

Look for opportunities to assist a friend or neighbor — mowing their lawn, shoveling snow, or carrying groceries — without waiting for them to request help.

At Work

1. Celebrate Colleagues

Recognize a coworker's accomplishments with a kind note, a compliment in a meeting, or a celebratory gesture like bringing in snacks for the team.

2. Volunteer for Unnoticed Tasks

Take on a less desirable task, such as cleaning up after a meeting or covering for a colleague, and do it cheerfully.

3. Give Credit Freely

Acknowledge others' contributions in team settings, even if it means sharing credit for a success.

4. Practice Gratitude

Thank a colleague or supervisor for their hard work, even if it goes unnoticed by others.

In the Community

1. Pay It Forward

At a coffee shop, grocery store, or drive-thru, pay for the person behind you. Add a kind note, such as "Have a great day!"

2. Volunteer Locally

Join a food pantry, animal shelter, or community cleanup program. Serve with no expectation of recognition or thanks.

3. Give Anonymously

Donate to a cause, provide groceries for a family in need, or leave a gift card for someone struggling financially — all without revealing your identity.

4. Extend a Warm Welcome

Introduce yourself to a new neighbor or a visitor at church. Offer to show them around, invite them to join a group, or simply provide a listening ear.

With Strangers

1. Practice Patience

The next time you're in a frustrating situation — like waiting in a long line or dealing with customer service — respond with kindness and understanding instead of irritation.

2. Offer a Helping Hand

Hold the door open, help someone carry a heavy load, or assist an elderly person or parent with young children.

3. Smile and Greet

Make eye contact, smile, and greet strangers you encounter during your day. A simple "Good morning" or "Have a nice day" can brighten someone's mood.

4. Leave Encouragement Behind

Write uplifting messages on sticky notes and leave them in public places, such as a library, café, or park bench, for strangers to find.

Spiritually Focused Practices

1. Pray for Others

Dedicate time each day to pray for someone who might never know you prayed for them. Include strangers, colleagues, or people you find difficult to love.

2. Fast for Others' Needs

Fast for a day and use the time you would spend eating to focus on praying for others' needs.

3. Practice Secret Giving

Find ways to give secretly, such as slipping money into an offering plate or leaving a care package for someone in need.

4. Meditate on Scripture

Reflect on verses about grace and love (see the Scripture Guide) and ask God to show you opportunities to live out these truths in your daily life.

Building Habits

1. Set a Weekly Goal

Each week, identify one specific act of one-way love to practice. Write it down, pray over it, and take action.

2. Keep a Gratitude Journal

Record moments when you gave or received unconditional love. Reflect on how these experiences deepened your faith and relationships.

3. Inspire Others

Share your experiences with practicing one-way love in conversations, small groups, or social media. Encourage others to join you in passing it forward.

These exercises are simple yet powerful ways to incorporate one-way relationships into your daily life. Start where you are, and trust that God will use your efforts to create ripple effects of grace and transformation.

About the Author

Hope Grace is a writer, translator, and advocate for faith-based living, whose work explores the transformative power of grace and unconditional love. Born in China and later immigrated to the United States, she brings a unique perspective shaped by her journey across cultures and her spiritual growth as a follower of Christ.

With a background in philosophy, divinity, and information science, Hope combines intellectual depth with heartfelt storytelling in her writing. She is the author of several works, including *Horizon Shift*, a thought-provoking exploration of humanity's resilience in the age of AI, and *From Passive to Passion*, her memoirs chronicling the journey she made from silence to activism as a Chinese immigrant.

Hope's passion lies in helping readers discover joy, resilience, and wholeness through one-way relationships and the grace of God. Through her work, she aims to inspire others to live with purpose, reflecting Christ's unconditional love in every aspect of life.

When she's not writing, Hope enjoys hosting Bible studies, mentoring others, and staying active on her fitness YouTube channel, *Age Gracefully with Hope*. She resides in Alexandria, Virginia, with her family. Learn more about her work at HopeGracePublishing.com.